EXTRAORDINARY
ANIMALS

AMAZING
SEA CREATURES

Andrew Brown

CRABTREE
Publishing Company

CRABTREE
Publishing Company

350 Fifth Avenue	360 York Road, R.R.4	73 Lime Walk
Suite 3308	Niagara-on-the-Lake	Headington, Oxford
New York, NY 10118	Ontario L0S 1J0	England OX3 7AD

Editor **Bobbie Kalman**
Assistant Editor **Petrina Gentile**
Designer **Melissa Stokes**

Illustrations by

Front cover: Steve Kingston (main), Elisabeth Smith, Valérie Stetten, Richard Tibbits; Back cover: Valérie Stetten

Mike Donnelly/WLAA (p. 10–11), Lee Gibbons (p. 6–7), Ruth Grewcock (p. 23), Steve Kingston (p. 16–17, 20–21),

Sandra Pond/WLAA (p. 8–9), Elisabeth Smith (p. 22–23), Valérie Stetten (p. 24–31), Kim Thompson (p. 18–19),

Richard Tibbits (p. 12–15), Simon Turvey, (p. 20)

Created by
Marshall Cavendish Books
(a division of Marshall Cavendish Partworks Ltd.)
119 Wardour Street, London, W1V 3TD, England

First printed 1997
Copyright © 1997 Marshall Cavendish Ltd.

Cataloging-in-Publication Data

Brown, Andrew, 1972-
Amazing sea creatures
(Extraordinary animals series)
Includes index.
ISBN 0-86505-561-0 (bound)   ISBN 0-86505-569-6 (pbk.)
1. Marine fauna – Juvenile literature.
I. Title.   II. Series: Brown, Andrew, 1972-   .   Extraordinary animals series.
QL122.2.B768 1997   j591.92   LC 96-46984

Printed and bound in Malaysia

CONTENTS

INTRODUCTION

Sea animals have special bodies that help them survive in the water. Fish have gills so they can live and breathe under water. Whales can dive deep into the water, but they must come up to the surface to breathe. Most sea animals have smooth bodies. Some have large, flat tails and flippers, which help the animal move easily through the water.

A DOLPHIN

has a smooth, thin body. It can shoot through the water like a speeding torpedo.

CRABS

have large front claws
that are used for catching
and opening shellfish—
the crab's favorite food.

SEALS

have very sensitive
whiskers on their face.
The whiskers help the
seal find food in deep,
dark water.

OCTOPUSES

can change color to match
their surroundings. This
helps the octopus hide
from hungry predators.

SEALS

Seals are found in every sea and ocean in the world, but most live in the cold waters of the Arctic and the Antarctic.

Millions of years ago, all seals lived on land. They belonged to the same group of animals as dogs, wolves, and bears. Over millions of years, the seal's body changed so the seal could live in the water. Scientists do not know why seals moved from land to water.

There are two kinds of seals—true seals and eared seals. True seals are covered with fine hair. They have smooth bodies to help them move easily through the water.

THE HEAD ▶▶▶

of the common seal has long, sensitive whiskers for finding prey. The seal has sharp teeth to help it hold onto slippery fish, which it swallows whole.

Since true seals do not have fur, they need another way to keep warm in the cold water. Seals have a thick layer of fat under their skin. It is called blubber, and it keeps them warm.

True seals usually stay in the water. Their legs are ideal for swimming. On land, however, it is difficult for seals to move. Seals come ashore to have babies or shed their hair. Each year, true seals shed all their hair and new hair grows in its place.

▲▲▲ THE BACK LEGS are used to push the seal through the water.

◀◀◀ THE FRONT LEGS are short flippers. When it swims, the seal keeps its front legs near its body. It uses its front paws to hold food.

OCTOPUSES ▶▶▶
are among the seal's favorite foods. Seals also eat fish, crabs, and penguins. Sometimes they even eat other seals!

Eared seals are much bigger and stronger than true seals. They are called eared seals because you can see their ears.

The California sea lion is one of the best known eared seals. It often appears in circuses, zoos, and aquariums around the world.

Eared seals have thick fur coats and large flippers. The flippers are so strong that the eared seals can use them to walk on land. They can move around on land more easily than true seals. Eared seals come out of the water often.

THE WALRUS'S TUSKS

1

2

(1) The male walrus's tusks can grow up to three feet (1 m) long. The walrus uses its tusks to pull its enormous body out of the water and onto the ice or rocks.

(2) The tusks are also used to make breathing holes. The walrus chips away ice and then hooks its tusks through the holes when it is resting or sleeping underwater.

(3) When the walrus looks for food, it uses its tusks to shovel shellfish off the seabed into its mouth.

3

◄◄◄ MALES
use their large tusks to fight one another. Sometimes the animals are seriously injured.

MANATEES

Manatees are gentle, harmless animals. They live in the warm waters of Florida, the Caribbean, the northern coast of South America and west Africa.

Manatees are sometimes called "sea cows" because they spend all day eating huge amounts of sea grasses. The manatee's appetite is so large that people bring them in to eat underwater plants that block rivers and canals. The manatees quickly eat their way through the plants, making it easier for people to move through the water.

Manatees stay underwater most of the time, but they must come to the surface every 15 minutes to breathe.

THE FLIPPERS ▲▲▲
are short. Manatees use them to move along the seabed, to push food into their mouth, and to touch other manatees.

THE TAIL

Manatees have a wide, flat tail that is shaped like a paddle. The tail is large compared to the rest of the manatee's body. The manatee moves its tail up and down to push itself through the water.

▼▼▼ THE SKIN

is usually gray or brown. It is very rough. Sometimes the skin is covered with scars from injuries caused by boat propellers.

DUGONGS

The dugong lives in the waters of Asia and east Africa. It has small eyes, a large, flat snout, and rough, brown skin. Even though the dugong looks like a big seal, its closest relative—next to the manatee—is the elephant!

The dugong is very shy and gentle. It usually eats at night when there are few animals around.

Sometimes the dugong is also called the "sea cow" because it grazes on water plants called sea grasses. The dugong eats a lot—it can eat one-tenth of its weight each night!

◀◀◀ THE DUGONG has very small teeth. It has hard pads on the roof of its mouth to grind tough water plants.

BOWHEAD WHALES

THE HEAD ▼▼▼

of this whale is smooth. The nostrils, or blowhole, are on top of the whale's head.

There are two main types of whales—toothed whales and baleen whales. The bowhead whale is a baleen whale.

Baleen whales do not have teeth. They strain their food through comblike, hard plates called baleen. The baleen hangs down from the roof of the whale's mouth. There are small gaps between each plate.

When the whale is hungry, it swims through the water with its jaws wide open. Once its mouth is full of water, the whale closes it. Water can escape, but any small creatures that are inside the mouth are trapped. Each day, the bowhead whale eats more than two tons of fish!

▲▲▲ **THE TAIL**
pushes the whale forward in the water. It has no bones, but lots of muscles.

BLUE WHALES

The blue whale is the largest animal that has ever lived. It measures almost 100 feet (30 m) long—about the same length as 17 adult humans lying head-to-toe! The blue whale's tongue is also large—it weighs as much as an elephant!

The blue whale is another type of baleen whale. Its favorite food is a type of tiny shrimp called krill. When it eats, the blue whale dives deeper in the water and swims back up straining fish from the water through its baleen.

THE BLOWHOLES ▼▼▼
are the whale's nostrils. The whale uses its blowholes to breathe and smell. It needs to come to the surface to breathe air.

During the summer, the blue whale stays near the North and South Poles, where there is lots of krill. In winter, the whale swims to warmer waters. There is less food in the warm waters, so the blue whale lives off its own thick layer of blubber!

Humans have hunted the blue whale for centuries. Up to 1930, humans killed more than 30,000 whales each year. The blue whale's blubber was used to make lamp oil, soap, and even explosives. Its baleen was used to make jewelry. In parts of southeast Asia, whale meat is a very popular food. Even though whale hunting is banned in most countries, some people continue to hunt whales.

▲▲▲ THE SKIN

is smooth and hairless. It allows the whale to move easily through the water. A thick layer of blubber under the skin keeps the whale warm.

◀◀◀ THE THROAT

has pleats, or grooves. The grooves stretch to help the whale take in massive amounts of water.

SPERM WHALES

The sperm whale is the largest type of toothed whale. It lives all over the world, except in the coldest waters of the Arctic and Antarctic. Sperm whales swim in groups called pods. During the year, they travel great distances looking for food.

The sperm whale has a very large head. Most of the head is filled with a waxy liquid called spermaceti. The whale uses the spermaceti to float and dive. Not long ago, people killed whales for their spermaceti. They used it to make cosmetics and candles.

A GIANT OF THE SEA

The sperm whale is the most powerful meat-eater on earth. It grows up to 70 feet (20 m) long. The sperm whale weighs ten times more than Tyrannosaurus Rex, or as much as 1,800 ten-year-old children! The sperm whale has the largest brain of any animal—it is the size and shape of a basketball and weighs over 15 lb (7 kg)!

THE SQUID ▲▲▲

is the sperm whale's
favorite food. The giant
squid above is a vicious
fighter. Many sperm whales
bear scars caused by the
squid's tentacles.

21

DOLPHINS

Dolphins are another type of toothed whale. They live in almost every ocean and at the mouth of some rivers.

Some people think that dolphins are fish, but they are not. Dolphins are mammals. People are mammals, too. Mammals need to breathe air. Dolphins breathe through a blowhole on the top of their head. The blowhole closes when the dolphin swims underwater.

▲▲▲ THE MOUTH

of the dolphin can have as many as 250 sharp teeth! The dolphin uses its teeth to grab fish—the dolphin's favorite food.

THE FLIPPERS ▲▲▲

are like paddles. They are used to steer the dolphin through water. Each flipper has five finger bones, which are covered with smooth skin.

HOW A DOLPHIN FINDS ITS FOOD

When a dolphin wants to catch prey, it uses its excellent sense of sound. The dolphin makes a series of clicking noises in its blowhole. These clicks travel through the water until they hit a fish. Then they bounce back to the dolphin like an echo.

If the sounds bounce back quickly, the dolphin knows that the fish is nearby. If they take longer, then the fish is farther away.

◄◄◄ THE BODY

is long and smooth. It is designed to help the dolphin move quickly through the water.

SALMON

Salmon live in the north Atlantic and Pacific Oceans. Every year, when salmon are ready to have their babies, they make long journeys from the ocean back to the rivers and lakes where they were born. This journey is called migration.

Before migration, the salmon eat a lot of food because they will not eat during the trip. Some salmon, such as the Atlantic salmon, make this long and difficult journey several times. Sometimes they swim over 200 miles (320 km)! Many salmon do not even make it—they are often eaten by other animals during their journey.

▲▲▲ **THE LOWER JAW** of the male Atlantic salmon changes to a hooked shape during the fish's long migration.

Once the salmon have reached the waters where they were born, the females lay thousands of eggs. Not all the young salmon will survive, but the ones that live swim back to the ocean waters.

▼▼▼ THE ADULT

Atlantic salmon below grows
up to 4 feet (120 cm) long and
weighs 12 pounds (5 kg)!

▼▼▼ THE BACK

of the salmon is blue with black
spots. The male's sides are silver,
but during migration they turn red.
The female's sides turn black.

OCTOPUSES

The name octopus comes from the Greek word *okta*, which means eight. The octopus has eight long arms, or tentacles. Each tentacle is covered with hundreds of suckers.

The octopus usually looks for food at night. When the octopus hunts, it sneaks up to a crab or fish and then wraps its tentacles around the prey.

When the octopus is attacked, it stretches out its tentacles and changes color to match the seabed. It also shoots ink at its attacker. If the attacker grabs one of its tentacles, the octopus will deliberately break off the tentacle. Then a new tentacle will grow in to replace the broken one.

OCTOPUSES AND HUMANS

Octopuses are very shy animals. They will not attack people unless they have been threatened first.

Some people think that octopuses wrap their arms around humans and squeeze them to death. This is not true. Some types of octopus, however, can be very dangerous. They have poisonous, deadly bites!

THE BODY ▼▼▼

is soft and muscular. It contains all the octopus's organs—a brain, heart, liver, and stomach.

THE TENTACLES ▼▼▼

can grow up to four feet (1.2 m) long. The octopus uses them to catch prey.

◄◄◄ THE SUCKERS

lie in rows on the tentacles. They are very sensitive. The octopus uses them to feel and taste different objects.

CRABS

Crabs are crustaceans. Crustaceans are animals that have a crust, or shell. The shell covers and protects the crab's head and body. The crab's legs are also covered with a similar hard shell.

Most crabs live in water, but some also live on land. When crabs come ashore, they do not walk in a straight line. They move sideways, pushing with the legs on one side of their body and pulling with those on the other.

The crab has big claws on its two front legs. It uses the claws to catch food and defend itself. The fiddler crab has one claw that is much larger than the other.

As the crab grows, it molts, or sheds, its shell. A new shell grows in a few days. While the shell grows, the crab is totally defenseless.

ALL CRABS ▶▶▶
have ten legs. Some crabs
have large back legs that they
use as paddles when they swim.

▼▼▼ **THE SHELL**
of this crab is about eight
inches (20 cm) wide.

CORALS

Corals look like plants, but they are tiny living animals that hunt and eat.

Corals are easily attacked by other animals. For protection, the corals group together and attach themselves to rocks. Then they slowly build a home called a coral reef. As more corals are born, they attach onto the top of other corals and the reef grows larger.

During the day, the corals stay closed. At night, they come to life. Each coral has tentacles. The corals stretch out their tentacles to look for food. Any small animals that swim into the tentacles are killed by the coral's powerful sting.

Coral reefs come in many different shapes and colors. The largest is the Great Barrier Reef on the northeast coast of Australia. It is 1,500 miles (2,000 km) long.

◀◀◀ **THE REEF**
is very hard, but it can be
easily damaged by humans
and boats.

◀◀◀ **THE CORALS**
stay inside the reef if they
sense danger.

INDEX

GLOSSARY

aquarium – a tank or pond in which living fish and other water animals are kept and watched

explosive – a substance that can blow up

prey – an animal that is hunted by another animal for food

scientist – a person who is an expert in nature and the universe

shellfish – an animal that has a shell and lives in water. Shrimps, lobsters, and clams are shellfish.

squid – a sea animal that has a round, tubelike body and ten arms

sucker – an organ on animals, such as octopus and squid, used for sucking or attaching to something

whiskers – the long, stiff hairs that grow near the mouth of animals such as seals, cats, and dogs